NEOCAPITALISM ACCORDING TO MICHEL CLOUSCARD

An Introduction

NEOCAPITALISM ACCORDING TO MICHEL CLOUSCARD

An Introduction

Aymeric Monville

TRANSLATED BY PHILIPPE GENDRAULT
FOREWORD BY GABRIEL ROCKHILL

First English Edition Published by *Iskra Books* 2023
Originally French Edition Published by *Les Éditions Delga* 2011

All rights reserved.
The moral rights of the author and translator have been asserted.

Iskra Books
www.iskrabooks.org
Madison, Wisconsin
U.S. | U.K.

Iskra Books is an independent scholarly publisher—publishing original works of revolutionary theory, history, education, and art, as well as edited collections, new translations, and critical republications of older works.

ISBN-13: 978-1-0881-8804-0

British Library Cataloguing in Publication Data
A catalogue record for this book is available from the British Library

Library of Congress Cataloguing-in-Publication Data
A catalog record for this book is available from the Library of Congress

Cover Art by Ben Stahnke
Cover Design and Typesetting by Ben Stahnke

Contents

Preface \ i
Aymeric Monville

Foreword \ iv
Gabriel Rockhill

Marxism Renewed \ 1

Marshall, Here We Come: From the Marshall Plan to Monopolistic State Capitalism and Markets of Desire \ 6

Consumer Society, Whose? \ 11

Anthropological Training \ 16

From the "District" to the New "Middle Classes" \ 25

May 1968, Beginning of the *Reconquista* \ 30

Popular Resistance \ 33

Preface to the First English Edition

Aymeric Monville

After a recent translation in Spanish, thanks to the publisher Iskra and professor of philosophy Gabriel Rockhill, the English-speaking public now has a faithful translation of this short work, which was the first essay to present the work of Michel Clouscard, a French thinker ignored by the Parisian intelligentsia for a quite some time (the bedrock of the so-called "French Theory"), but whose work has now managed to spread throughout the world. This is precisely one of his many points in common, biographical, and theoretical, with Jean-Jacques Rousseau.

Clouscard is anchored in certain realities of France and in the long historical experience of its labor movement, which, in my opinion, are amply explained in this presentation and in the editor's notes. However, make no mistake: Clouscard understands Marxism too well not to constantly focus his national analysis on that of the capitalist mode of production as a whole, which has followed the same trajectory—from the conservative and fascist society of penury to the current generalized crisis, passing through the mirage of libertarian liberal social democracy (a concept we owe to Clouscard), as permissive towards the consumer as it is repressive towards the producer. In this sense, Clouscard understood his time. He was certainly the Honoré de Balzac of neocapitalism.

Capitalism went through three fundamental stages to reach an illusory cruising speed: after the traditional liberal competitive capitalism—which was not idyllic either, as it was perfectly suited to slavery and child labor in the mines—came an imperialist, colonialist, national socialist phase which wanted to represent the exacerbation of all that—"the terrorist dictatorship of the bourgeoisie," in Dimitrov's terms; and finally, after the Marshall Plan, came a phase of compromise with neocapitalism and a new model—always equally repressive towards the producer, but more permissive towards the consumer.

It is at this point that the dominant ideology spoke of the so-called "consumer society," which is nothing more than the society of those who can consume the labor of others.

All this with a new form of mind control and seduction that Pier Paolo Pasolini aptly described as a now "total" form of fascism.

The illusions of redistribution, of growth, of social progress in a capitalist system are dissipating today in many parts of the world. The bourgeois king is naked and today, more than ever, we are faced with the alternative: socialism or barbarism.

Freud was convinced that he was bringing the 'plague' to America. Michel Clouscard's antidote to the "French Theory," of which there is not a single author to whom he has not opposed from a Marxist point of view, will undoubtedly be perceived as another plague. We know the ambiguity, in ancient Greek, of the word φάρμακον (*phármakon*), which could mean "remedy," "drug," "philter," as well as "poison" or "venom." It is up to the reader to decide, according to their sensibility, their class affiliation and which fate they wish for the world and its children.

A. M., January 2023

French Communism versus French Theory

An Introduction to Clouscard & Monville

Gabriel Rockhill

In this book, Aymeric Monville provides us with a concise and insightful overview of the work of a major French Marxist: Michel Clouscard. Unfortunately, his writings are almost completely unknown in the Anglophone world. Due to a series of factors, some of which Clouscard himself deftly diagnosed, the global theory industry has promoted anti-communist French theory—as well as forms of Marxism opposed to actually existing socialism—at the expense of thinkers like Clouscard and Monville. This is a direct consequence of U.S. cultural and intellectual imperialism, which has been the driving force behind the phenomenon known as French theory.

It is an honor to collaborate with Iskra Books in this effort to democratize the circulation of intellectual production and bring to the Anglophone world such an important work. Since Monville is a major intellectual, editor and activist in his own right, this translation has the advantage of spotlighting the research of two major Francophone Marxists. Moreover, Monville is in many ways the ideal guide to Clouscard's expansive body of writings, which he has worked through assiduously. Although there are many major insights to be found in them, Clouscard's writings are often more suggestive and provocative than demonstrative and pedagogical. Monville's framing and presentation of his work thereby brings clarity and precision to his project. For the purposes of introducing it to an English-speaking audience, I would like to outline in what follows a few of the most relevant and significant contributions made by Clouscard and, by extension, Monville.

Toward a Marxist Theory of Consumerism

Clouscard has provided an astute analysis of the consumer dynamics operative in postwar capitalist countries, with a particular focus on France. He foregrounds, in particular, the importance of the Marshall Plan, a U.S. imperialist project that injected billions of dollars into Western Europe ($12 billion between 1948 and 1951 according to

Monville, which is the equivalent of $150 billion in 2023).[1] This investment, 23% of which was directed to France, sought to keep the region within the U.S. sphere of influence, preserving and further developing its capitalist economy as a bulwark against the heightened post-WWII risks of communism. Defining the potlatch as "an extravagant expenditure that allows for the establishment of social hierarchy according to consumption," Clouscard writes: "The potlatch is born [in France] from the Marshall Plan. The bourgeois consumption specific to neocapitalism begins with the penetration of American imperialism. The Americanization of French life is inaugurated by the consumption of the surpluses *made in USA* [in English in the original]."[2]

Unlike many other accounts of so-called consumer society, Clouscard pays particular attention to the class polarization at work in contemporary capitalist countries. He completely rejects the idea, found in the work of Herbert Marcuse and others, that the working class simply sold out and lost any revolutionary potential it might have had. He also lambasts the concomitant assumption, which has

---

[1] These stats are from the current book and can be found below.

[2] Michel Clouscard. *Le Capitalisme de la séduction: Critique de la social-démocratie libertaire* (Paris: Éditions Delga, 2015), 37-8. Unless otherwise indicated, all translations are my own.

been widespread in certain sectors of the so-called New Left, that the true revolutionary force in society is to be located outside of the proletariat, in the middle-class stratum, including the students and youth who were born into it or aspire to it. This self-aggrandizing anti-worker politics narcissistically and naively confers upon the libertarian consumers of this middle layer the role of revolutionaries.[3]

What the expression 'consumer society' tends to obscure is the fact that there is only one class stratum that gets to truly indulge in consumerism, which is precisely the petty-bourgeois layer that was—in the case of France—bolstered by the Marshall Plan. Its members are the ones who have the means to revel in the marketplace of desire and in worldly and fashionable (*mondain*) consumption, which is reserved for the privileged few. While they do not own the means of production, and do not therefore have access to anything like the life of luxury of the bourgeoisie, they can nonetheless, at their own scale, participate in an urbane and cultured lifestyle of libertarian consumerism. Rather than buying out of sheer need, they consume based on desire, which extends above and beyond what is

---

3 See, for instance, Aymeric Monville. *Les Jolis Grands Hommes de gauche: Badiou, Guilluy, Lordon, Michéa, Onfray, Rancière, Sapir, Todd et les autres...* (Paris: Éditions Delga), 2017, 37.

necessary or even useful.

Clouscard thereby provides what Monville calls a "phenomenology of ideology."[4] He describes, in minute detail and with some remarkable insights, the daily lives of those who participate in the marketplace of desire. Putting the lie to those who foolishly proclaim that Marxism only analyzes the macro-dynamics of society and is incapable of describing the micro-dynamics of everyday life, Clouscard pursues a tradition that can be traced back to Friedrich Engels' *The Condition of the Working Class in England* and Karl Marx's *Economic and Philosophic Manuscripts of 1844*. The focal point for Clouscard's phenomenology of the subjects of capitalism is, however, the new petty-bourgeois class stratum in the imperialist core since approximately WWII.

Clouscard provides a dialectical analysis of this stratum by always situating it in relationship to the working class. Whereas the former is free to consume, the latter is subjected to repressive relations of production. The dream of Western consumerism has been internationally promoted by the Marshall Plan and other imperialist projects to bait Western Europeans into supporting capitalism. It has also served the all-important purpose of fostering aspirational desire on the part of people across

---

4 Ibid., 38.

the global South and within socialist countries. All of these populations are directly targeted by the US-based dream machine with the mendacious message that they too could, thanks to the magic of capitalism, have a carefree lifestyle of self-indulgent consumerism.

Seductive Capitalism & the Nightmare of Production

Although it was made in a very different context, Fernando E. Solanas and Octavio Getino provided a striking visual depiction of these producer-consumer dynamics in the first part of their three-part film *La hora de los hornos* [*The Hour of the Furnaces*] (1968).[5] The sequence entitled "Dependency" opens with a nearly seamless series of slow, circular aerial pan shots depicting the cityscape of Buenos Aires while a voiceover explains that the history of Latin American countries has been "the history of an endless colonial looting." "The labor of a people reduced to cheap manpower," the narrator explains, "has built the wealth of the great powers. In this exploitation lies the cause of the backwardness, poverty, oppression, which in turn guarantee the financing and high living standards of the rich na-

---

5 See Fernando E. Solanas and Octavio Getino. *The Hour of the Furnaces*, 1968, https://www.youtube.com/watch?v=jQOXKoMHOE0 (accessed on February 2, 2023).

tions, and here lies the origin of that obscure word invented by imperialism: underdevelopment." As this last word is pronounced, the sentence is visually punctuated by a dramatic visual descent into the dark world of slaughterhouses where laborers are hard at work, which starkly contrasts with the gleaming skyline of the capital port city just depicted. The visible capitalist development of the city is thus revealed to be built upon the concealed world of labor.

The montage sequence in the slaughterhouses that follows juxtaposes workers killing animals with seductive still images that look like advertisements promoting the so-called American way of life, viz. well-to-do people indulging in consumer goods like cars, cigarettes, soft drinks, liquor, chocolate, cosmetics, and so on. Meanwhile, intertitles recall the realities of imperialist underdevelopment, stating for instance: "every day we work more in order to earn less." After the workers succeed in bludgeoning the cattle to death with a sledgehammer, the camera zooms in on a cow's twitching eye, which appears to be looking up, as if at a movie screen. A still image of this eye captures the moment of death, and then the ads suddenly *come to life* by becoming moving images. It is as if the dead eye of the animal was gazing upon a screen depicting scenes of consumerist joy and smoky seduction: a stylish couple embracing, frolicking women in bathing suits, a man excited to be behind the wheel of a shiny truck, a woman with a drink blowing a come-hither kiss.

This is a perfect cinematic depiction of Clouscard's thesis, with an important imperial twist. The carefree life of libidinal consumerism for the privileged few is dialectically dependent upon the repressive life of labor for the many. The rhythm of the entire sequence plainly communicates, moreover, that it is not only the cattle that are being beaten over the head. The workers themselves are being bludgeoned with advertising images of a cheerful and seductive life, which is so tantalizingly close that they might be able to reach it (if they just worked harder). The audiovisual message is crystal clear: like the animals they are forced to cudgel, workers are themselves beasts of burden hammered with the propaganda of the ruling class and its advertising industry. As a matter of fact, as the final sequence demonstrates, the more the workers are beaten into death-like submission and stultified by illusions, the more the dream of consumerism *comes to life* for the lucky few.

Very much like Clouscard, Solanas and Getino remind us that the so-called American dream of Western consumer society is only for a privileged layer of the population. Furthermore, it is by no means an accident that this class segment is situated in the capitalist core—with extensions in the comprador class in the periphery—since its global socioeconomic standing is a consequence of imperialism. Its rank is most definitely not for everyone, and the workers of the world are well positioned to recognize this, in spite of all of the propaganda to the contrary. For them, the dream of Western consumerism is actually an extended nightmare. They can and do fantasize about being able to freely consume what they produce, like those above them in the socio-economic order, but this could only occur under socialism. Within the capitalist system, they can consume in even a limited manner only if they submit themselves to repressive labor conditions and accept to be the slaves of the system.

Jean-Pierre Levaray, a worker and writer interviewed in a documentary film on Clouscard, explains this situation with a remarkable juxtaposition. Discussing Clouscard's account of contemporary France, he says: "It's the society we live in; it's capitalism. You can go everywhere; you can go to Seychelles. You can have a super big, polluting four-wheel drive and all. You can do that. But it's going to be complicated to have it. You are going to have to crawl. You are going to have to submit. You are going to have to accept all our norms."[6] The

---

6 Ossian Gani and Fabien Trémeau. *Tout est permis mais rien n'est possible: Un documentaire sur la pensée de Michel Clouscard* (2011): https://editionsdelga.fr/produit/tout-est-permis-

fantasy of libertarian consumerism is thus actually, for the workers, a nightmare of exploited labor.

This is the system that Clouscard refers to as "capitalism of seduction" or "libertarian liberalism."[7] Freedom for the petty-bourgeois consumer is conjoined with repression for the producer. What the blanket term *consumer society* erases, then, is the class polarization between "those who consume more than they produce" and "those who produce more than they consume."[8] Moreover, as Monville explains, working-class consumption according to Clouscard amounts to the struggle to equip oneself with consumer items that themselves have become necessary for the reproduction of the labor force. In the case of France, this includes things like a vehicle to get back and forth to work, a refrigerator to preserve food, a stove to cook for oneself, etc. This type of social-reproductive consumerism, Clouscard points out, is just a second form of exploitation, and it is markedly distinct from the libertarian consumerism of the petty-bourgeoisie. Workers, to be competitive on the labor market, need to purchase the means of efficiently repro-

---

mais-rien-nest-possible/ (Accessed: February 25, 2023). A version of the film with English subtitles is available here: https://www.youtube.com/watch?v=So7AJEYQY4U (Accessed: February 25, 2023).

7 Monville, *Les Jolis Grands Hommes de gauche*, 33.

8 These quotes are from the current book.

ducing themselves day in and day out, and getting themselves back and forth to work.

This situation is aptly summarized by Clouscard in his pithy and penetrating description of seductive capitalism: "everything is allowed, but nothing is possible [*tout est permis, mais rien n'est possible*]."[9] Contemporary capitalist society has been characterized by an expansion of libertarian consumerism for one class layer, which indulges in the end of prohibitions and taboos (everything is allowed). However, this unfettered consumerism is dialectically dependent upon an increasingly repressive sphere of production, which shackles the working class (nothing is possible). It is this dialectic that structures contemporary capitalism: the middle layers pursue the reverie of liberation through chic cosmopolitan consumerism, while the workers are ensnared in the horror of exploitative production.

Third Way Politics & Culturalism against Class Analysis

Clouscard, as Monville shows, provides a perspicacious analysis of the dominant ideology of the petty-bourgeois class stratum in the imperialist core. One of its tendencies is to embrace third way politics, which is characterized by the belief in a so-

---

[9] Michel Clouscard. *Néo-fascisme et idéologie du désir* (Paris: Éditions Delga, 2017), 130.

cio-economic and political system that would neither be purely capitalist nor socialist. Such a third way can be inflected in slightly different directions, but what they all share is a refusal to accept the very core of class struggle, namely the irresolvable contradiction between two classes: the bourgeoisie and the proletariat.

Since there is not actually a third way, meaning that it is not possible to resolve the contradictions of capitalism other than through socialism, third way politics is ultimately just a circuitous path to capitalist accommodation (even if capitalism ends up being reformed in some capacity). Moreover, Clouscard describes a shift from what he sees as the local fascism of the extreme right in the early 20th century to what he refers to as a global fascism or neo-fascism in the latter part of the 20th century. In this new form of fascism, the petty bourgeoisie accepts the brutal destruction of human life unleashed around the world by the likes of institutions such as the International Monetary Fund and the World Bank. After all, this class stratum, as noted above, materially benefits from imperialism, so it is nowise surprising that it ideologically supports it.[10]

---

10 Zak Cope has done some important research on this topic in his books *The Wealth of (Some) Nations: Imperialism and the Mechanics of Value Transfer* (London: Pluto Press, 2019) and *Divided World Divided Class: Global Political Economy and the*

In addition to the tendency to embrace third way politics and support neo-fascism, another feature of the political orientation of the petty-bourgeois class stratum is its preponderant concern with the societal (*le sociétal*) at the expense of the social (*le social*). Societal issues are those related to questions of morals and values, often in relationship to individual rights; whereas social issues relate to the composition of society as a whole and, in particular, its class dynamic. In the Anglophone world, and more specifically in the United States, this distinction is closest to the difference between culture wars or culturalist politics, on the one hand, and class analysis on the other. Clouscard's work can thus be understood as being in dialogue with—though at a slight distance—many of the excellent Marxist critiques of the new petty-bourgeois class stratum's embrace of identity politics and culturalism as a bulwark against class politics.[11]

Michael Parenti has provided a memorable critique of the most important aspect of this culturalist approach to politics in his account of what he

---

Stratification of Labor under Capitalism (Montreal: Kersplebedeb, 2015).

11   Adolph Reed Jr. has been one of the most persistent, insightful, and intrepid critics of identity politics as a class project (see his book *Class Notes* or many of his other publications). Ellen Meiksins Wood, William I. Robinson, Salvador Rangel, and Jennifer Ponce de León have also made very important contributions on this front.

called ABC Theory: Anything But Class. "Many who pretend to be on the Left," he writes, "are so rabidly anti-Marxist as to seize upon any conceivable notion except class power to explain what is happening. They are the Anything-But-Class (ABC) theorists who, while not allied with conservatives on most political issues, do their part in stunting class consciousness."[12] Directly inspired by Parenti, I have emphasized in my own work how ABC theorists, and even many self-proclaimed Marxists, indulge in ABS Theory when they seek to correct societal or social problems: Anything But—actually existing—Socialism. They put forth myriad solutions that dismiss out of hand socialist state-building projects in the real world. ABS Theory is thus ultimately A BS Theory, meaning a theory that is BS: it does not provide the tools necessary for successfully fighting against imperialism or materially addressing the root causes of purportedly cultural problems like racism, misogyny, homophobia, etc.

The Counter-Revolutionary 68 Thinkers

The global consumer phenomenon known as French theory has been integral to the international promotion of a coterie of trend-setting intellectuals: Michel Foucault, Jacques Derrida,

---

12 Michael Parenti. *Blackshirts and Reds* (San Francisco: City Lights Books, 1997), 145-146.

Hélène Cixous, Jacques Lacan, and many others. These figures have been marketed in the larger English-speaking world as radical, transgressive, innovative, and unorthodox. One aspect of this has been their symbolic affiliation with the uprisings of May 68, and in particular the student movement in Paris. This association has led many to believe that French theory is somehow inherently radical and represents an insurgent assault on institutionalized knowledge akin to the students storming and occupying the Sorbonne.

As I have documented in a forthcoming article, those marketed as '68 thinkers' were disconnected from and generally dismissive of the historic workers' mobilization.[13] With few exceptions, they were also hostile to, or at least skeptical of, the student movement. They were, for the most part, anti-68 thinkers, or at a minimum, theorists who were highly suspicious of the demonstrations. Foucault, to cite one of the most flagrant examples, actually served on the governmental commission responsible for the Gaullist academic counter-reforms that were one of the most important triggers for the student movement. He was thus very clearly positioned on the opposite side of the barricades and widely recognized at the time as a Gaullist techno-

---

13 See Gabriel Rockhill. "The Myth of 1968 Thought and the French Intelligentsia: Historical Commodity Fetishism and Ideological Rollback." *Monthly Review* (June 1, 2023).

crat and an institutional operator, as well as a "violent anti-communist."[14]

Clouscard provides us with a much-needed corrective to the widespread free association between French theory and 1968. He highlights how there were in fact two movements at work. On the one hand, there was the workers' mobilization and the struggle for real gains for the working class, which he supported. On the other hand, there was the student and youth insurgency, whose leaders showed many signs of embracing petty-bourgeois libertarian third way politics and the promotion of the societal over the social. While many of the students voiced criticisms of capitalism, they often conjoined these with a rejection of actually existing socialism, as well as a belief in a new revolutionary subject (not the proletariat). It is the student and youth mobilization, with its spectacle of revolution in the Latin Quarter, that has been retained by bourgeois history and widely affiliated with French theory.

1968 was thus indeed a turning point in French

---

14 Didier Eribon. *Michel Foucault* (Paris: Flammarion, 1989), 237. For more on Foucault's opportunism and anti-communism, see Gabriel Rockhill. "Foucault: The Faux Radical." *Los Angeles Review of Books*, "The Philosophical Salon" (October 12, 2020), https://thephilosophicalsalon.com/foucault-the-faux-radical/ (accessed on February 2, 2023).

history, but it was not revolutionary in the positive sense of the term. Although there were some gains for the working class, the primary consequence of 68 for Clouscard was the decline of the two forces of anti-fascist resistance—communism and Gaullism—as well as the rise of Atlanticism. At the end of *Néo-fascisme et idéologie du désir*, he describes 68 in terms of a psychodrama at the summit of the state. Three leading figures served as the symbols of possible ideological systems: "the stern father (de Gaulle), the *enfant terrible* (Cohn-Bendit), the debonair liberal (Pompidou)."[15] The form of French society that emerged in the wake of 68 was one in which the liberalism of Pompidou (the Prime Minister in May 68 and then the President of France as of 1969) allied with the libertarianism of the anti-communist student leader Cohn-Bendit to oust the conservatism of traditional French society (personified by de Gaulle). 68 thereby marked the advent of "libertarian liberalism" and the consolidation of a social order that was permissive and libertarian in the realm of consumerism but repressive in the sphere of production.

It is in this light that the marketing of French theory qua 68 thought makes sense. Although the most visible French intellectuals—affiliated with structuralism and so-called post-structuralism—generally turned their backs on the movement or

---

15 Clouscard, *Néo-fascisme et idéologie du désir*, 128.

expressed their skepticism, in the wake of 68 they were widely promoted, and often presented themselves, as radical, anti-Establishment free spirits à la Nietzsche. Outside of a few partial and usually short-lived exceptions, they were opposed to actually existing socialism, even though they sometimes voiced criticisms of capitalism. Their discourses were thus often in tune with the third way politics of libertarian liberalism and the privileging of the societal over and against the social. Their market niche was precisely the new petty-bourgeois class stratum in the imperial center—and those who aspire to it—which tends to indulge in consumerism as a means of liberation while shunning the socialist project.

To take but one telling example, Derrida unequivocally proclaimed: "I cannot construct finished or plausible sentences using the expression *social class*. I don't really know what *social class* means."[16] As if his subjective limitations simply coincided with objective reality per se, he dismissed class analysis out of hand, while apparently remaining ignorant of the fact that such a rebuff is itself a classic shibboleth of the petty-bourgeois class stratum. Furthermore, relying on a shamelessly incorrect stereotype concerning "the econo-

---

16 Jacques Derrida. *Negotiations: Interventions and Interviews, 1971–2001*, trans. Elizabeth Rottenberg (Stanford: Stanford University Press, 2002), 170.

mist dogma of Marxism," Derrida went on in the same interview to berate the Marxist tradition for its supposed lack of conceptual and discursive refinement, professorially prescribing that "some engagement with Heidegger or a problematic of the Heideggerian type should have been mandatory."[17] Instead of trying to force Marxists to engage with the work of an unrepentant Nazi, perhaps this lesson giver should have done a bit of close reading of any of the countless critiques of economism within the Marxist heritage. At a minimum, the French master of suspicion could have questioned his spontaneous subjective ideology—as a member of the petty-bourgeoisie in the imperial core—concerning the category of class, opening up his professorial mind to learning from those who are 'totally other' than the members of his Heideggerian clique. Amílcar Cabral, for instance, could surely have helped Derrida learn to use the expression *social class*: "the socio-economic phenomenon 'class' is created and develops as a function of at least two essential and interdependent variables—the level of productive forces and the pattern of ownership of the means of production."[18] Mao Zedong could have assisted the French theorist in understanding

---

17 Ibid., 170, 173.

18 Amílcar Cabral. "The Weapon of Theory," 1966, https://www.marxists.org/subject/africa/cabral/1966/weapon-theory.htm, accessed on February 26, 2023.

that his skeptical attitude toward the category of class is actually a very precise signifier of his class standing: "In class society everyone lives as a member of a particular class, and *every kind of thinking, without exception, is stamped with the brand of a class*."[19] Finally, the magus of deconstruction could have learned something about the primacy of objective reality over subjective intuition from the likes of Walter Rodney. He cogently explained that the Ghanaian leader Kwame Nkrumah "denied the existence of classes" like Derrida "until the petty bourgeoisie as a class overthrew him"—at which point he was forced to recognize that classes do indeed exist.[20]

Returning to Clouscard, and borrowing from his punchy formulation, we could say that the mantra of French theory is: '*theoretically* everything is allowed, but *practically* nothing is possible' (i.e., the capitalist system cannot be fundamentally altered). The theoretical practice of this segment of the French intelligentsia is characterized by unbridled postmodern play, intellectual syncretism, rhetorical pyrotechnics, a consumerist fetishization of difference, a frenetic proliferation of bourgeois

---

19 Mao Zedong. *Collected Writings of Chairman Mao*. Vol. 3. *On Policy, Practice and Contradiction*. El Paso: El Paso Norte Press, 2009, 22, my emphasis.

20 Walter Rodney. *Decolonial Marxism*. London: Verso, 2022, 48 (also see 68-69).

cultural references, and an overall ethos of breaking taboos and prohibitions in order to indulge in a veritable bacchanalia of free-floating theory. The marketing of these intellectuals as '68 thinkers' can thus be seen as part of the new petty-bourgeoisie's consumerist utopia, where radicality is symbolic and can be purchased in the form of transgressive theoretical products (which serve as an ersatz for concrete engagement in revolutionary politics).

Strictly speaking, the so-called 68 thinkers were those whose careers were buoyed by the rising tide of radical consumerism in the wake of 68, which was driven by a very strong current of libertarian anti-communism. Their rhetorical and theoretical capers were promoted as a revolution in theory where it had failed in practice. Symbol thereby sought to replace substance. Through a process of historical commodity fetishism, the events of 68 were repackaged for their exchange-value, independently of the actual social relations operative at the time. Instead of theory with real use-value for the struggles of working people, here was a theory that played no concrete role in the events of 68 but instead recuperated their symbolic value post factum to augment its radical cachet, and hence its exchange-value in the marketplace of desire.

The overwrought discourses of the French theorists are, in fact, those of revolutionary failure.

Gilles Deleuze was categorical on this front: "All revolutions fail [*foirent*]. Everyone knows it: we pretend to rediscover it here [with the reactionary anti-communist writings of André Glucksmann and François Furet]. You have to be a complete idiot [*débile*] [not to know that]!"[21] Failure in this regard corresponds to the success of the counter-revolution. In the case of post-68 France, and more specifically its intellectual scene, the counter-revolution meant the displacement of Marxism—a philosophy celebrated in postwar France for having successfully led the colossal effort to stop the Holocaust and defeat fascism—by imperious philosophies of radical suspicion marketed as new, edgy, unconventional, and *absolutely different* (than Marxism).[22]

It is noteworthy in this regard that Deleuze, Foucault, and Cixous were interlocutors with the French government for its project of creating the experimental University of Vincennes in the wake of 68, which became a veritable bastion for radical

---

21 P.A. Boutang, *L'Abécédaire de Gilles Deleuze*, 2004, transcribed here: https://www.oeuvresouvertes.net/spip.php?article910, accessed on February 27, 2023).

22 On the practice of consumerist differentiation, which fundamentally structures the theoretical practice of the so-called philosophy of difference, I take the liberty of referring the reader to my text "Is Difference a Value in Itself?" in *Interventions in Contemporary Thought: History, Politics, Aesthetics* (Edinburgh: Edinburgh University Press, 2017), 117-138.

theory (Foucault, Cixous, Deleuze, Lacan, Jean-François Lyotard, Alain Badiou, Étienne Balibar, Jacques Rancière, and Félix Guattari all taught there at some point). Jean-Pierre Garnier, a sociologist interviewed in the Clouscard film mentioned above, reports that he heard Pompidou make the following claim: "All these people, the famous 'restless ones [*les agités*]', if we give them classrooms, if we give them amphitheaters, they will make their revolution in a vacuum, and during this time, we will have peace in the street."[23]

At more or less the same time, the Minister of the Interior—and former Vichy official—Raymond Marcellin began a long campaign of counter-insurgent repression. He forbade protests during the next elections and invoked a 1936 anti-fascist law to ban eleven leftist organizations, while simultaneously allowing the extreme Right to act with impunity (including violent movements like Occident). This marked the onset of years of widespread censorship of leftwing publications, dragnet identity checks to filter out and deport leftist foreign nationals, the emboldening of fascist commando units, and draconian measures targeting the Left like the 1971 prohibition on *any* public meeting or protest "*susceptible* to disturb public order."[24]

---

23 See Gani and Trémeau, *Tout est permis mais rien n'est possible*.

24 Maurice Rajsfus. *Mai 68: Sous les pavés, la répression (mai*

The contrast could not be clearer: whereas the fashionable French theorists were given a platform for their theoretical tempests in teapots, those who were dedicated to changing the world—instead of endlessly interpreting it—faced widespread repression.[25]

1968-mars 1974). Paris: le cherche midi éditeur, 1998, 206, my emphasis. Some of the numbers cited by Rajsfus are worth mentioning in order to provide a sense of the scale of the repression: 1,035 leftists received prison sentences between 1968 and 1972, 890 people were arrested for distributing left-wing tracts between November 1969 and March 1970, and in 1970 there were 1,284 citations against leftists (*ibid.*, 240, 140, 147).

25 There are, of course, some significant differences between the theorists who taught at the University of Vincennes, which would later become the University of Paris 8. For instance, figures like Balibar and Badiou moved in Marxist theoretical circles early on, and Lyotard was in *Socialisme ou barbarie* until 1964. As their careers evolved and then blossomed internationally due largely to promotion in the U.S., they tended—like the other theorists who had engaged in more leftist politics at some point—to drift away from revolutionary theory and engage more with fashionable discourses like deconstruction (Balibar), the philosophy of difference (Lyotard), or Lacanian psychoanalysis and metaphysics (Badiou). The latter is a partial exception to this rule insofar as he was a social democrat before 68, and he persists in referring to himself as a Marxist today, and more specifically a Maoist. This is because he is an outspoken supporter of specific elements in the Chinese Cultural Revolution, not unlike those who see in it a liberatory attack on the state and the party. Unsurprisingly, then, he nonetheless condemns other socialist state-building projects, including contempo-

It is worth noting, moreover, that these repressive measures were nowise restricted to France. The strategy of tension, a policy according to which terrorist violence is encouraged and even instigated by the state, was implemented across Western Europe in the wake of 1968. The objective was to blame the violence on the Left, use it as a justification for raiding and attempting to destroy communist organizations, create an ambiance of insecurity and pave the way for popular support for authoritarian and even fascist governments. Federico Umberto D'Amato, who "started in the Secret Services of the police forces and the Ministry of the Interior in the Fascist era" and continued "in the anti-Fascist era," in the words of Vincenzo Vinciguerra, has spoken openly about this in Allan Francovich's outstanding documentary *Gladio*.[26] After the 1968 events in France, D'Amato explained, "there was a real threat posed by subversive elements in Europe so I proposed we set up a permanent committee, a European committee [...] called the Berne Club." This club brought together "all the secret services of Europe and America," according to Vinciguerra. They had been collaborating on Operation Gladio,

---

rary China, thereby revealing his proximity to the dominant 'anti-totalitarian' ideology.

26 See Allan Francovich. *Gladio*, 1992, available here: https://www.youtube.com/watch?v=yCvEgQ3HSQ0 (accessed on March 10, 2023).

which consisted in setting up secret NATO stay-behind armies across Europe that were trained and controlled by the CIA and MI6. For the strategy of tension, these armies—often stocked with Nazis and fascists—were activated and committed a long and bloody list of false-flag terrorist attacks against the civilian population that were blamed on communists. In 2020, the Bologna public prosecutor's office concluded that D'Amato, a.k.a. the Godfather, was one of the four instigators, organizers and financiers of the 1980 Bologna train station bombing that left 85 dead.[27] This was only one of many such attacks, and the Italian parliamentary commission investigating Gladio concluded in 2020: "Those massacres, those bombs, those military actions had been organized or promoted or supported by men inside Italian state institutions and, as has been discovered more recently, by men linked to the structures of United States intelligence."[28] These operations were not restricted to Italy, as the official Italian Senate investigation into Gladio concluded in 1995: "It emerges without the shadow of a doubt that elements of the CIA start-

---

27 See the article "Strage di Bologna, chiuse le indagini: 'Bellini esecutore, Licio Gelli mandante'" in *Sky TG24* (February 11, 2020): https://tg24.sky.it/cronaca/2020/02/11/strage-bologna-bellini-gelli (accessed on March 10, 2023).

28 Cited in Daniele Ganser. *NATO's Secret Armies: Operation Gladio and Terrorism in Western Europe* (New York: Frank Cass, 2005), 14.

ed in the second half of the 1960s a massive operation in order to counter by the use of all means the spreading of groups and movements of the left on a European level."[29]

Having studied French theory for decades—including under the direct guidance of intellectuals like Derrida, Irigaray, and Badiou—I have never come across a single reference to Operation Gladio, NATO's secret stay-behind armies or even the repressive anti-communist policies of Marcellin in the work of any of the French so-called masters of suspicion (even though some of the revelations regarding the fascist stay-behind armies started to trickle out into the mainstream press as early as 1952). These purported critics of all forms of power were also silent on the Central Intelligence Agency's intellectual world war on communism, including the explosive 1966 revelations that the Congress for Cultural Freedom (CCF) was a CIA front. The CCF was a global anti-communist propaganda organization headquartered in Paris, where it worked hand-in-glove with the intellectual don of anti-communism—and Pierre Bourdieu's early mentor—Raymond Aron. Bourdieu is the only French theorist who even mentions the CCF, as well as its French journal *Preuves*, as far as I know. However, in a disingenuous attempt to whitewash history, he omitted the fact that the

---

29 Cited in ibid., 81.

CCF and *Preuves* were CIA fronts that globally promoted Aron, the man who had secured Bourdieu his first foothold in the academy and the stewardship of an elite research center.[30] Promotion for some, repression for others: this is the dialectic of material forces at work behind the cultural imperialist consumer product known as French theory.

French Theory: Made in the USA

The Ford Foundation played a central role in launching French theory as a global phenomenon. It funded, with a massive grant of $36,000 (338,000 dollars in 2023), the 1966 international conference at the Johns Hopkins Humanities Center, which is largely recognized as having inaugurated the era of French theory.[31] Explicitly organized as a beachhead in North America for European structuralism (including what would later be called 'post-structuralism'), it brought together, for the first time in

---

30 See Bourdieu's preface to Brigitte Mazon. *Aux origines de l'E.H.E.S.S.* Paris: Les Éditions du Cerf, 1988, I-V.

31 Some of the details concerning this event, as well as a selection of the presentations and discussions, are available in Richard Macksey and Eugenio Donato, eds. *The Structuralist Controversy: The Languages of Criticism and the Sciences of Man* (Baltimore: The Johns Hopkins University Press, 1972). More information can be found in Stuart W. Leslie. "Richard Macksey and the Humanities Center." *MLN* 134:5 (December 2019): 925-941.

the U.S., leading luminaries from the Francophone theoretical scene. Derrida met Lacan there for the first time, as well as his future collaborator Paul de Man. Roland Barthes, René Girard, and Tzvetan Todorov were all present, and Deleuze sent in a paper. Foucault could not join in person, but he served on the advisory board for the symposium. As Richard Moss reported: "Since there were no Marxists present (except, perhaps, Lucien Goldman) and since the bourgeois ideologists, other than the structuralists themselves, were observers, the controversy was primarily between various tendencies within the structuralist school."[32] This had the effect of presenting what would become known as 'French theory' as a non-Marxist intellectual trend.

Representatives from the Ford Foundation (Sigmund Koch) and the Carnegie Foundation (Peter Caws) were both present at the Hopkins symposium, and there was a closed-circuit television channel to accommodate the overflow from the standing-room-only crowd. In a move almost never seen in the academy, *Time* and *Newsweek* actually sent correspondents to report on the event, which received "widespread press coverage from mainstream newspapers and magazines in the U.S. [...] and in France, *Le Monde* and *The Partisan Re-*

---

32 Richard Moss. Review of *The Language of Criticism and the Sciences of Man*. *Telos* 6354-6359 (1970), 354.

view."[33] *Time* and *Newsweek*, it is worth recalling, had deep ties to the U.S. National Security State. "According to CIA and Senate sources," writes Carl Bernstein, "Agency files contain written agreements with former foreign correspondents and stringers for both the weekly news magazines."[34] Henry Luce, the founder and editor-in-chief of *Time* and *Life*, was a close collaborator with the CIA and a personal friend of CIA Director Allen Dulles.[35] Luce's "personal emissary to the CIA was C.D. Jackson," who served as the vice-president of *Time* and was "an unofficial minister for propaganda with almost unlimited powers."[36] *The Partisan*

---

33   Leslie, "Richard Macksey and the Humanities Center," 933.

34   Carl Bernstein. "The CIA and the Media." *Rolling Stone* (October 20, 1977).

35   "Like the *New York Times*," Hugh Wilford writes, "Henry Luce's weekly [*Time*] provided CIA officers with journalistic credentials [...]; Dulles laid on regular dinners for *Time* foreign correspondents similar to those he gave for CBS, receiving in return post-assignment debriefings and favorable publicity; and the Luce organization would come to the assistance of other magazines whose circulation figures did not match its own yet were considered worthy causes by the Agency, such as *Partisan Review* and the *New Leader*" (*The Mighty Wurlitzer: How the CIA Played America* (Cambridge, Massachusetts: Harvard University Press, 2008, 231-232).

36   Bernstein, "The CIA and the Media"; Frances Stonor Saunders. *The Cultural Cold War: The CIA and the World of Arts and Letters* (New York: The New Press, 2000), 147. In the early

Review received essential funding from Luce and was published by the U.S. chapter of a CIA front organization: the American Congress for Cultural Freedom (ACCF).[37] It certainly appears, then, that

---

1950s, Saunders goes on to write, Jackson "did more than any other to set the agenda for American cultural warfare" (*The Cultural Cold War*, 148). Documents available at the Eisenhower Memorial Library provide remarkable insight into the depth and breadth of the U.S. government's propaganda apparatus and C.D. Jackson's central role in it. This apparatus, according to many documents, specifically targets opinion makers like professors, journalists, and political leaders with "doctrinal warfare" aimed at countering communist philosophy with a defense of so-called free world ideology. A document dated March 28, 1956, which resulted from an Operations Coordinating Board working group, spells out 21 pages of talking points that can be used to purportedly refute all of the major themes of Marxism, from its account of capitalism and imperialism to its positions on the national question, bourgeois democracy, colonialism and much more (Edward P. Lilly Papers, 1928-1992, Box 55, Folder "Doctrinal Programs 1956-1964"). Another document I found, the Operations Coordinating Board's "Outline Plan of Operations for the U.S. Ideological Program," provides a 14-page overview of the coordinated efforts on the part of multiple agencies (State Department, DOD, USIA, FOA, CIA) to develop their doctrinal war against communism through international exchange programs, seminars and colloquia, the production and global distribution of ideological materials, the utilization of private organizations and groups, and more (Edward P. Lilly Papers, 1928-1992, Box 55, Folder "Ideological Education: Freedom Academy: Militant Liberty").

37 Regarding Luce's bailout of *The Partisan Review*, see

there was some interest in mobilizing press assets in an endeavor to promote non-Marxist theory from Western Europe.

The Ford grant obtained by Hopkins also underwrote the publication of papers from the 1966 symposium and the appointment of a distinguished international scholar as a visiting faculty member. The conference inaugurated, moreover, a two-year program of continuing seminars, colloquia, and numerous other activities. Barthes, Derrida, Foucault, and Charles Morazé subsequently led graduate seminars at Hopkins. Derrida was hired as a half-time visiting professor, and de Man joined the full-time faculty. All of this led to an intensification of Transatlantic intellectual exchanges that internationally promoted the work of non-Marxist—and often openly anti-communist—Francophone theorists.[38] In the cases of Derrida and de Man,

---

Saunders, *The Cultural Cold War*, 162-163. On *The Partisan Review* more generally, see, in addition to Saunders' book, Patrick Iber. "Literary Magazines for Socialists Funded by the CIA, Ranked." *The Awl* (August 24, 2015) and Giles-Scott Smith and Charlotte A. Lerg, eds. *Campaigning Culture and the Global Cold War: The Journals of the Congress for Cultural Freedom* (London: Palgrave Macmillan, 2017).

38 As Stuart Leslie explains, Yale soon surpassed Hopkins as one of the primary hubs for these trans-Atlantic intellectual exchanges (and the University of California at Irvine later came to play an important role). "In 1972," Leslie writes, "Yale literary critic Geoffrey Hartman, who had been

to take but two relevant examples, it is worth recalling that the former would go on to be directly involved in subversion efforts against Czechoslovakia, co-founding the French chapter of the Jan Hus Educational Foundation to support the work of anti-communist dissidents. De Man, who would later regularly invite Derrida to Yale, had worked and written for three publication platforms in Belgium that collaborated so closely with the Nazis that their directors were all sentenced to death in the wake of WWII. As a matter of fact, the maestro of deconstruction was so tight with the Nazi collaborationist publishing world that he apparently expected to become a minister of culture in the European Reich after the war.[39]

---

on the list of alternates for the [Hopkins] symposium speakers along with his then Cornell colleague Paul de Man, hired away de Man, Miller, and Derrida and so 'signaled the moment when 'the Hopkins School' became the 'Yale School,'" the place where deconstruction would flourish for a generation (Macksey, "Letter to Suskind"). The Ford Foundation, taking stock of its investment, conceded that financial crisis at Hopkins in the early 1970s and the defections of key faculty had put the Center on life support, but that it nonetheless represented an important model of interdisciplinary inquiry worthy of future support" (Leslie, "Richard Macksey and the Humanities Center," 936).

39 Evelyn Barish's biography of de Man, based on "years of original archival work and over two hundred interviews," provides a particularly damning portrait of one of Derrida's closest collaborators: *The Double Life of Paul de Man* (New York: Liveright Publishing Corporation, 2014).

The President of the Ford Foundation at the time of the famous Hopkins symposium was McGeorge Bundy. He had just served as the U.S. National Security Advisor and was a major operator in the U.S. national security state. He had previously collaborated with Allen Dulles and Richard Bissell of the CIA in studying the use of Marshall Plan funds by the Agency to finance anti-communist propaganda activities. Part of the history of the Marshall Plan, which is an important complement to Clouscard's work, is that the CIA was using funds tethered to it to finance psychological warfare operations in Western Europe. As Kai Bird explained in his book on McGeorge and William Bundy:

> The CIA was tapping into the $200 million a year in local currency counterpart funds contributed by the recipients of Marshall Plan aid. These unvouchered monies were being used by the CIA to finance anti-communist electoral activities in France and Italy and to support sympathetic journalists, labor union leaders and politicians.[40]

The Ford Foundation, like the other major capitalist foundations, has a long and deep history of working closely with the CIA, particularly on these types of projects. For instance, it funded, alongside the Agency, the international anti-communist propaganda organization mentioned above: the Congress for Cultural Freedom (CCF). The CCF has been described by Hugh Wilford as "one of the

---

40 Kai Bird. *The Color of Truth: McGeorge Bundy and William Bundy: Brothers in Arms* (New York: Touchstone, 1998), 106.

most important artistic patrons in world history, sponsoring an unprecedented range of cultural activities, including literary prizes, art exhibits, and music festivals."[41] It was the exact same year as the Hopkins conference that the CCF was revealed to be a CIA front. In a shambolic and short-lived effort to save face, the Ford Foundation took over the funding of the CCF and renamed it.

These are but some of the material forces of anti-communist cultural imperialism that have been at work behind the global phenomenon of French theory. I have had the opportunity, in my own research, to foreground other dynamics, notably pointing out that the CIA explicitly identified structuralism as an asset in its anti-communist propaganda endeavors.[42] This is also true of the

---

41 Wilford, *The Mighty Wurlitzer*, 101-102.

42 See, for instance, Gabriel Rockhill. "The CIA Reads French Theory: On the Intellectual Labor of Dismantling the Cultural Left." *Los Angeles Review of Books*, "The Philosophical Salon" (February 27, 2017), https://thephilosophicalsalon.com/the-cia-reads-french-theory-on-the-intellectual-labor-of-dismantling-the-cultural-left/ (accessed on February 17, 2023) and Gabriel Rockhill. "Foucault, Anti-Communism & the Global Theory Industry: A Reply to Critics." *Los Angeles Review of Books*, "The Philosophical Salon" (February 1, 2021), https://thephilosophicalsalon.com/foucault-anti-communism-the-global-theory-industry-a-reply-to-critics/ (accessed on February 17, 2023). For additional information on the history of the U.S.'s propaganda activities in the cultural Cold War, also see Gabriel Rockhill. *Radical History*

Annales school of historiography, represented at the Hopkins symposium by the participation of Charles Morazé, as well as the fact that the Humanities Center in Baltimore was largely modeled on the Sixième Section of the École Pratique des Hautes Études. This latter institution, funded by the Rockefeller Foundation and directed by Fernand Braudel, was known as the epicenter of the *Annales* school. It actively participated in all stages of the planning of the 1966 conference at the Humanities Center. In a 1985 CIA research paper that explicitly references the importance of the work of Foucault and Claude Lévi-Strauss, the Agency states: "Although both structuralism and *Annales* methodology have fallen on hard times (critics accuse them of being too difficult for the uninitiated to follow), we believe their critical demolition of Marxist influence in the social sciences is likely to endure as a profound contribution to modern scholarship both in France and elsewhere in Western Europe."[43]

Following Clouscard, Monville has provided, in his own work, an important overview of the anti-dialectical and anti-communist orientation

---

& the Politics of Art (New York: Columbia University Press, 2014).

43 "France: Defection of the Leftist Intellectuals," 6: https://www.cia.gov/readingroom/document/cia-rdp86s00588r000300380001-5 (accessed on February 2, 2023).

of many of those who have been internationally promoted as major French theorists. They are the ones who opportunistically gave to the U.S.-driven system of intellectual production what it demanded, and they have received handsome rewards in return. For instance, as Monville points out in his book on 'left Nietzscheanism,' Deleuze very explicitly rejected Marxism qua class analysis in *Dialogues*, which is a position that he shared with Foucault. Monville recalls how the latter embraced Nietzsche and Heidegger at the expense of Marx, while also focusing on the question of power instead of property. The author of the current book also skewers Derrida for revealing "the key to his entire corpus" in an oracular pronouncement that unwittingly sums up French theory as a U.S.-driven imperial cultural product: "deconstruction is America [*la déconstruction c'est l'Amérique*]."[44] Derrida's elusive signifiers are actually *open to*—Marxist—*interpretation*, for once!

Monville has pursued his Clouscardian critique of French theory, and the global theory industry more generally, by extending it to include some of the latest hot commodities on the radical theory shelf, such as the work of Alain Badiou, Jacques

---

44 Aymeric Monville. *Misère du nietzschéisme de gauche: De Georges Bataille à Michel Onfry* (Bruxelles: Éditions Aden), 2007, 80.

Rancière, and Slavoj Žižek.[45] Monville's position aligns with that of Domenico Losurdo in *Western Marxism*, a work whose themes overlap with those of the current book.[46] Losurdo, whom Monville has translated into French, is another major figure in European thought whose scholarship, like Clouscard's, is anchored in and develops the Marxist tradition over and against anti-communist radical theory (which is sometimes marketed as 'Marxist').[47] All three of these figures are representative of the fact that *there is an alternative* to the theoretical practices promoted by the global theory industry.

---

45 See Monville, *Les Jolis Grands Hommes de gauche*.

46 The English translation of this important work is forthcoming from Monthly Review Press.

47 Although figures like Badiou and Žižek often self-describe as Marxists, or even communists, the devil is in the details of their work. As I have argued, they are both ultimately utopian socialists (at best, particularly in the case of the reactionary Žižek). They regularly turn their noses up at actually existing socialism—with the noteworthy exception of the Cultural Revolution for Badiou—in favor of a purported "Idea" of communism or a "desire" for it. See Gabriel Rockhill. "Capitalism's Court Jester: Slavoj Žižek." *CounterPunch* (January 2, 2023), https://www.counterpunch.org/2023/01/02/capitalisms-court-jester-slavoj-zizek/ (accessed on February 25, 2023).

For a Democratization of French Theory

Monville and Clouscard are part of a tradition of French thought whose international visibility has suffered from the consequences of U.S. cultural imperialism. Like the other theorists in this tradition, such as Georges Gastaud, Annie Lacroix-Riz and many of the other authors published by Éditions Delga (which is run by Monville), they do not fit within the anti-communist marketing niche of French theory. Their work has therefore largely been judged to be unworthy of English translation and commentary by those who own and control the means of intellectual production and circulation. Most, if not nearly all, of those Anglophone consumers who pride themselves on being knowledgeable of French theory, or even professional experts in the field, have no clue who they are.

Yet, they represent one of the most important theoretical traditions in contemporary France. Unlike the opportunist intellectuals who acquiesced to the uplift from the U.S.-driven theory industry, adapting their discursive production to the demands of the system, these theorists have humbly toiled away. They have made major contributions to the collective project of elucidating the social totality and providing a framework for both understanding and transforming the material world.

They have rejected the dominant anti-communist ideology, and they have also stood firm against the opportunities for professional advancement that result from subservience to capitalist-driven theoretical trends and the concomitant rejection of Marxism, and more specifically Leninism.

If their work were widely available in English and a regular part of contemporary debates, we would have a sense of what French theory might look like in a world less dominated by U.S. cultural imperialism. It is therefore a great pleasure to collaborate with Iskra in struggling against these imperial forces in order to contribute to a substantive democratization of theory. Hopefully other translations will follow so that English readers will no longer be deprived of this crucial work.

NEOCAPITALISM
ACCORDING TO
MICHEL CLOUSCARD

Marxism Renewed

If Marxism has continued to inspire countless thinkers, Michel Clouscard included, it has certainly not been because Marx was endowed with any particular ability to predict our present days, but because Marx carried his analysis of capitalism to such a level of critical abstraction that, in its quintessence, many of his observations remain valid today.

Both our own time and Marx's time are characterized by the same mode of production, namely capitalism. Accordingly, we could say that Marx's time is also ours.

Of course, within capitalism, numerous phases and periods can be distinguished. In order to proceed with a renewal of Marxism, then, we must first understand the present state as well as capitalism's general strategy. This must be done because this particular mode of production is in constant evolution consequent to its fundamental contradictions, starting with, most importantly, the contradiction between the private aspect of *ownership* of the means of production and exchange and the growing collectivization or socialization of production set up by necessity.

This contradiction creates tremendous imbalances, contrary to what the liberal economic school, posterior to Marx, has said. The liberal economic school dreams of a pure and undistorted competition, of an equilibrium between offer and demand, of an invisible hand regulating society's imbalances without intervention by public institutions.

The terrible crises of the twentieth century have given a significant amount of import to Marx—and what is to come, it appears, will not refute his work either. Marx, himself, conceived of the possibility for capitalism to temporarily minimize some of its own contradictions, which, most characteristically, is the tendency of the falling rate of profit. Such 'solutions' are not lacking: an increase in the rate of exploitation, the worldwide expansion of imperialist markets, immense crises of devaluation due to wars, the rise of the welfare state in an effort to avoid the crisis of overproduction, etc.

Michel Clouscard was born in 1928 and passed away in 2009. From the crisis of the thirties to our contemporary crisis—which may, in fact, be one and the same—Clouscard lived through the many phases of capitalist development in France. As an adult, he witnessed the country's transformation by the Marshall plan, as well as its effects in 1968, and the victory of what Clouscard had called "libertarian social-democracy," and the general crisis of the state.

Clouscard witnessed many phases of the alternation between crisis and recovery. With this tremendous *fool's game* characterized by a so-called "consumer society"—that is, a society of those who consume a greater portion of the products of labor than they themselves produce—some have tried to impose the idea that this form of society somehow represented an "end of history"; that capitalism had reached its cruising speed following the tacit agreement of May 68—that is to say, for the right to manage the economy and for social-democracy to manage only the "societal," an emancipation from traditions and customs, an emancipation that cost capital nothing, and an emancipation which allowed for the creation of new markets. Nothing, of course, prohibits an implementation of the state's *iron fist* for those remaining defiant of this brave new world.

We are not dealing here with a form of capitalism fundamentally different from an older version, but instead with a specific strategy which remains to be decrypted. To such ends, the bypassing of a contemporary Marxist thinker like Clouscard seems deeply erroneous.

Doing so becomes impossible if one wishes

to exit the internal cycles of crises and 'recovery' found within capitalism and to propose a true alternative, which can be defined as the collective appropriation of the means of production and exchange, i.e., socialism, humankind reconciled with itself, and ready to confront the challenges that nature presents. This would be what Marx called humankind's "end of prehistory," an era which today seems to be made possible by technical progress; a perspective in front of which capitalism appears like a veritable impediment to the progress of productive forces. To qualify this impasse, Clouscard spoke of a "rotting of history," a quasi-obsession that ran throughout his work and which probably originated in the disappointment he felt after the disarmament of resistance partisans and the consequent conjuring away of the victory over fascism. (Clouscard himself was 17 in 1945). Despite all the sacrifices, capitalism in France and beyond remained as it was before; everything was free to start over again—fascism, colonialism, exploitation.

The majority of Europe's World War II resistance fighters did not say "no more war," but understood the situation with far more political nuance, echoing J. Jaures, and instead calling for "no more capitalism, a system that carries war like a thundercloud." Partisan nuance set up powerful national precedents of socialization, even in countries more heavily aligned with the western side.

It is, of course, not by chance that the former second-in-command of the MEDEF,[1] Denis Kessler, stated that the National Council of the Resistance had to be terminated and that, in Italy, the postwar "Republican Constitution" must be the object of every attack from employers and management.

To enable this new "corruption of history"—a veritable counter-revolutionary restoration, and "the change of everything that would lead to no change at all," after the corruption of the trenches, the corruption by fascism, and the ruin of history—minds had to be broken. Whatever could be bought ought to be, and the rest had to be crushed. Thus was the final blow of the Marshall plan.

---

1 MEDEF (*Mouvement des Entreprises de France*, or Movement of French Enterprises) is an organization of French business owners.

Marshall, Here We Come: From the Marshall Plan to Monopolistic State Capitalism & Markets of Desire

The Marshall plan was, before all else, a 12-billion-dollar infrastructure investment given by the United States, between 1948 and 1951, to 16 European countries: 23% for France—of which 83% was gifted and 17% was lent.

These massive gifts had two goals: one was to impose the American way of life, and to discourage social subversion, but the other was to prevent the pending crisis of overproduction and to get the machine working again—and to eventually guarantee new markets. In Marxist terms, if the war allowed for a devaluation of the capital necessary to avoid a panic caused by the decrease in profit rate and the intensification of social conflicts, the Marshall plan would help prevent the crisis of overproduction by providing another outlet.

Capitalism, in order to find some illusory cruising speed, went through three fundamental phases. To the classical liberal competitive capitalism (which is far from perfect; let's recall it took no issue whatsoever with young children slave-laboring in mines) succeeded an imperialist, colonialist, and a national-socialist phase, with all the intensification these phases represented ("the terroristic dictatorship of the bourgeoisie" according to Dimitrov).

Following these appeared a phase of compromise, with neocapitalism introduced by the Marshall plan—a new model, repressive, as usual, towards the producers, but now far more permissive towards the consumer. Today, after the disappearance of the pressure exercised upon capitalism by world socialism, we might speak, along with Jean Ziegler, of a so-called "re-feudalization" of the world.

After the erasure of the revolution of 1917, the same needed to be done with the revolution of 1789. France, since 1789, has been the site of an uncompleted revolution. The revolution has been incomplete because, in part, of the on-going conflict between the republic and liberalism. In Great Britain and the United States, liberalism prevailed; the *Glorious Revolution* had witnessed the alliance of the monarchy and the bourgeoisie—and in the United States specifically, the alliance of slave owners and political white supremacy. This is the liberalism of the happy few, of deals between friends.

Since August 10, 1792 (the storming of the *Palais*

des Tuileries, and the fall of the constitutional monarchy), France saw a new kind of development: an anti-liberal, progressive, historical bloc carried forward by the Jacobins, opposed to the commercialism of the Gironde and to slavery, proposing a fair distribution of lands, universal suffrage, and the defense of the nation. Let us not forget that, prior to the Jacobins, the bourgeoisie thought to carry out the revolution for its own benefits; such was the spirit of the decree of *Allarde,* which suppressed corporations, or of the law *Le Chapelier,* which banned organizations and gatherings of workers. *Thermidor* ended this, whereas the bourgeoisie had been seriously challenged, and brought the revolution back to something of a middle ground. Since then, France has been going through a contradictory, vacillatory process of movement—a back and forth, the republican reality, transposed onto a backdrop of the class struggle.

An appreciation of these historical considerations is necessary. In France, for example, the Marshall plan was attached to an ambiguous structure, centralized and interventionist, and characterized by a nation-state setup by the monarchy and the republic itself. The planning of the post-war period was, in fact, galvanized by the Marshall Plan. In large part, this was the reason why France, more so than others, directly embraced a form of monopolistic state capitalism—that is, capitalism as monopolies and monopolies as state management.

Monopolistic state capitalism is characterized by an unprecedented rise in productive forces and the total, even totalitarian, organization of the society born from it. Monopolistic state capitalism can be further characterized by:

1. maximal organization of production: that is, productionist exploitation through a maddening work pace and the extreme parceling out of labor (Fordism, Taylorism), along with near-ubiquitous threats of relocations or unemployment

2. maximal organization of space: that is, a rural exodus allowing the dispossession and real estate speculation over an area of leisure (tourism, country houses, etc.) as well as speculation in the area of labor (low-income housing, public transportation, etc.)

3. maximal organization of private life, of consumption, and social traditions

All of this is to say that the monopolistic capitalist state allows civil society—the so-called *wild beast*, mentioned by Hegel and used by Clouscard to title one of his books—to become unchained.

Indeed, through population displacements as well as through the organization of numerous collective and domestic machineries now necessary for the reproduction of labor forces and a new urbanization, monopolistic state capitalism produces both the *product* and the *customer*.

Prior to this phase, capitalism had been loosely satisfied with dictating *how* to produce. Now, however, it seeks to dictate *how* to consume. And, beyond that, how to live.

This dictatorial move has introduced transformations within the very heart of the ruling ideology of capitalism itself. The bourgeois value system of efforts and of savings must, therefore, be radically altered into the consumerist model—specifically for those who can consume!

Effectively, the Marshall Plan facilitated the emergence of a new market of desire, which in turn enabled the total reduction of desire itself to a type of market. It forged forth a society that was solely a market, permissive for the consumer in its lifting of taboo and prohibition, molded under the framework of capitalism, driven by distinct dual velocities.

After this quintessential phase of capitalism, that is to say *imperialism*, we can now speak of an even more ultimate phase: namely a final conquest of hearts and minds. This, according to Clouscard, represented a veritable "colonization" of republican France itself.

Consumer Society, Whose?

Clouscard, from the 60s on, opposed head-on the Marcusian chorus so dominant at the time: namely, that the working class would have sold itself out for a plate of soup and that its gains on a social level would, in a sense, reveal its gentrification.

The Marcusian discourse allowed for a conferral to the libertarian consumer characterizing the new middle social strata (the so-called middle class) a type of narcissistic "revolutionary" status, to the detriment of the French proletariat, who could now be accused of betrayal for not integrating into the "system." This of course was nothing other than a pathway for the accessing of mundane consumption—advertising for the system. The libidinal economy of Marcuse, or the "desiring machines" of Deleuze, are nothing other than the lifestyles of the social-climbers characteristic of the new profit system—desire as abstraction, cut off from production, and pertaining directly to phantasmatic propaganda.

The leaders of this process have introduced a transgressive model of consumption as *revolution-*

ary, even though it might only be described as the ambitiousness of the middle class. The slogans of May 68 leftists were quite explicit in that regard. "Be realistic; demand the impossible!" "Never work again!" Or, in other words: "Make others do the labor."

It is possible to witness, in some milieus, a social consumer; but we have yet to see a "consumer society." If, as Clouscard tells us, workers were able to access all the goods they produced, we would already be in a socialist society!

In his book, *Neo-fascism and the Ideology of Desire*, through a mode of analysis which is now quite well known, Clouscard demonstrated that the *Thirty Glorious Years* have allowed the working class to access, not so much consumer goods but the capital goods necessary to the process of capitalist production: for instance, cars to get to work, washing machine to facilitate the general systematizing of domestic labor, etc. To be clear, we can say that workers and employees, constituting the majority of the French population, do not consume, or at least consume very little; they in fact use different capital goods. "Consuming," in this sense, means going through to another order of class, which reveals a gratifying investment in which the working class does not have access—or access to very little of. Namely, a libidinal, ludic, and marginal consumption, a privilege of the bourgeoisie and, in part, of the new middle class.

This libidinal, ludic, and marginal consumption is certainly a "distinction," since workers and employees cannot quite access it, yet it is not essentially contrary to what Bourdieu's concept would have us believe: an unrestrained race towards snobbery, towards more refinement. Indeed, all bourgeois are not aesthetes. Far from it. At most, this refined distinction hides a much more brutal and binary distinction consisting in establishing a cut between two worlds; the world of those who consume more than they produce and the world of those who produce more than they consume. Before the French revolution, Chamfort spoke of "those who have more appetite than food for dinner, and those who have more food for dinner than appetite." Here, the transformation of the mode of production opposed, on the one hand, those who were allowed to self-satisfy through consumption and, on the other, those who were only able to consume for the sake of a reproduction of their labor force, who have acquired the goods now necessary for collective and domestic life to be sustained.

Workers and employees have therefore been exploited twice over, namely in production but also in consumption. They must consume to equip themselves in order to participate in the new organization of production, and to secure whatever else remains to be purchased in service of this. No matter what, they find themselves hammered down by inflation and the tax on added values, as profits can only ever be obtained by way of living, human labor. Hence, to thwart the crises of opportunity, leisure activities must also be exploited—and today, consumption itself. Further, none of this takes into account the neuroticizing of markets, a vestige of the nineteenth century's hysteria.

Today, the greatest irony is that supermarket customers are often required to check themselves out at self-service cash registers. This is sold as a ludic activity as, akin to the flipper of the pinball machine, the consumer has been conditioned to these quasi-automatic operations. The extraction of surplus value is spreading everywhere, to all customer operations and market exchanges.

Marxists ought to require themselves to reflect upon the domain of consumption, and to clarify the historical and dialectical laws of the process of consumption. We must insist on the originality of Clouscard's *applied* Marxism, of his articulation of social classes not only in terms of production but of consumption as well.

Clouscard refused to stay within the traditional representation of the nineteenth century proletariat in order to better demonstrate that exploitation had, in fact, mutated into other forms—forms which must be better understood, because, unfortunately, this very representation could be utilized to obscure and to hide contemporary forms of exploitation (a stone thrown into the pond of dogmatic Marxism). Provided, moreover, that needs are created by the modes of production, poverty therefore could only be determined through a perception of the whole. As Clouscard observed, "poverty driving a car is still poverty."

Such an organization of consumption fits quite well with so-called "French Theory," "Spirit of 68," and other contemporary byproducts—that is to say, the "promotional" exhortation of the new economy, in which we are basking today.

A new treaty needed to be forged between the bourgeoisie and that new middle class born from the Marshall Plan; but, as well, a veritable education—a training—of the population to the new distribution and consumption would have to be organized. That is, the creation of the love of consuming for some, and the dream of consuming for others.

Anthropological Training

Where the extreme left (here we use the term in the pejorative sense used by Lenin when he speaks of *left communism*) only sees political power as libidinal repression, Clouscard, with much more subtlety, demonstrated how political power transformed itself into seduction, thereby "inventing" and producing the libido—the right kind of libido (something Foucault took quite a while to appreciate!).

In this regard, the field of sensibility is covered up by ideology. It allows for the training of the body for consumption alone—from childhood, where the belief exists that it can be enough to press a button, thus leading to a belief in the naïve, spontaneous, peremptory use of products.

This is the automatic operation; we go from swinging to the unforgiving metric beat to better imitate the rhythm of labor. To obtain *jouissance*, we must therefore exploit our own selves. This is the production of an objective, social neurosis. All comers are incited into a semiologic, symbolic consumption; a consumption of signs emptied of their contents in order to create the need for the libidinal, the ludic, and the marginal—all without truly satisfying such a need. Take, for instance, the night club: the rhythm for which we swing, the sound system, and the blare.

As we mentioned above, France is a country where republic and capital confront each other. Thus, *Liberty, Equality, and Fraternity* must by necessity be opposed by the new coming capitalism and its strategy proper: the archaic, *Work, Family, and Homeland*; meaning *work* (exploitation), *family* (mafias against the republic), and *homeland* (in the nationalistic, aggressive sense of the term used by monopolies and gun merchants; the opposite of a nation threatened in the face of feudalism).

For Clouscard, in post-Marshall Plan France, and contra *Liberty, Equality, and Fraternity*, another ideology will be needed; namely *sex, drugs, and rock & roll* will be called forth.

In order to go from a "society of savings to a society that gets off," a whole psychodrama will be needed to foster a radical break from the old world; a veritable script will be required, new roles must be assigned, and models, sufficiently violent, must overwhelm traditional structures. This might be illustrated, for instance, by the adage, "living from hatred and from beer," or by breaking one's guitar on stage and dying at the age of thirty. Or again, one might embrace a more smarmy and insidious violence, living like a hippy on the backs of those who work. This latter figure illustrates the ideology of absolute consumption, consisting of the consuming and enjoying of the labor of others while not producing for oneself, in keeping all the mundane privileges offered by one's social circumstances, i.e., having one's cake and eating it too.

These various models find, today, an opportunity in the era of conviviality. Indeed, once the republic has been destroyed and once history itself has been forgotten, it becomes possible to invent not only new social ties but ties between us, within one's class: this is the ideology of the movement from street to *Facebook*.

There is then, today, a convergence towards some ahistorical, artificial pseudo-harmony—a truly virtual, technologically-informed, cybernetic paradise, where one can exhibit one's life in front of Big Brother, hoping to occasionally be invited to some "giant (virtual) cocktail party."

Clouscard already spoke of the conviviality of information technologies where one's alienation could be exchanged and bartered. From "spectacle" to reality television, only the exhibition of the particular; only the distinguishable, *solo numero*, to the generalization of a self-entrepreneurship model, thus leading to the shattering of the labor contract.

This techno-horizon leads to the erasure of conflicts and history, to the benefit of an imagined "naturalness"—of an ahistorical nature. Ecology has thus far been able to offer three presentations with regard to this: that of the "land, which does not lie," that of technological refusal under Heideggerian auspices, and finally, today, once the overall model has been secured, that of the bucolic pseudo-conviviality, of organic goods, of countrified homes, and of "green" capitalism.

Clouscard, who, in *Being and Code*, analyzed French society from feudal modes of production to contemporary ones, appreciated quite well that such a "nature" was nonexistent in France. A field is in fact a cleared forest. It is a nature which, for a long time, has been worked over, humanized, and then abandoned. It has been abandoned consequent to the rural exodus towards suburbia; an exodus today replaced by a reverse migration, a veritable green neo-colonization of the countryside. The back-to-the-land hippies, the faux-environmentalists, and the *bobo*[1]—even the *bobobo* (bourgeois, bohemian, and Buddhist)—transform desertification into bucolic landscaping, like so many scavengers of rural misery. The country home becomes, in such regards, the very emblem of a France born

---

1 **Editor's note:** In France, the term *bobo*, a portmanteau used to describe the bourgeois-bohemians, is used analogously to the term "champagne socialist" in the United States.

from the Marshall plan.

A *capitalism of seduction* plays out a hilarious scene bearing witness to the communion of the techno-manager and his left-wing son, both with their natural, healthy, organic values. Whereas in earlier times they might have speculated over the peasants' despair, after the psychodrama of May 1968, both father and son have reconciled on the backs of rural misery—upon the countryside dreamscape of parvenus and *les nouveaux riches*.

Thus does the exploitation of the producers' labor continue, while, at the same time, *les nouveaux riches* make sure to keep the producers, the "polluters," away!

This is the source of the old anger over those with paid vacations; an anger which seeks to ridicule the workers' class struggles to the benefit of the new societal struggles, often undertaken concurrently by those who have the gall to claim allegiance to the left. This is the case with environmental activist and former Minister of Ecology, Nicolas Hulot, who sought to show you amazingly beautiful landscapes—beautiful precisely because you are not, and never will be, in them.

As Marx's sixth thesis on Feuerbach states, quite substantially, there can be no human essence aside from the totality of the individual's social relationships. The converse would have you believing in some corporeal human essence, naturally good, and with legitimate needs, somehow transcendent of capitalist society's oppression.

Clouscard, on the contrary, suggested that desire was naught but the expression of specific modes of production; a notion which allowed for the avoidance of polemical obstacles over the false needs of the faux environmentalists.

There is no innocent desire and, perhaps more specifically, there is no innocent consumption. We consume a given *production*, and an extracted production at that; a historically-layered production; a state of nature worked over millennia; a state forged by the republic and the class struggle. Capitalism has invented an illusory innocence by creating a general state of historical amnesia, a complete monopolization of sensibility. It has us believing in an *elsewhere* of the very process of production, somehow existing prior to history and within its own signification. Clouscard named this the ideology of the *ante-predicative*, which posits the subject prior to all predicates, before any discourse, hinting at its real substance.

This is the ideology of a beginning, of the prehistorical, and of an innocence anterior to any mode of production. It is the nostalgia of a lost substance, which characterizes the very core of reactionary ideology.

Psychoanalysis plays its part as well in this ideology, precisely because the task of the Freudian unconscious is to cover up yet another unconscious—that of production. For instance, psychoanalysis only sees the father and not the owner, the person and not the patriarch. Such a position culminates in a Lacanian neo-nominalism, with its chains of signifiers cut off from all referents.

Ante-predicativism and neo-nominalism constitute the two foundations of this ideology, indicative of both a time prior to and outside of production. We can bring up, for example, Roland Barthes for whom fashion was an ensemble of homogenous signs *outside* society, i.e., with regard to critique, the text might now be studied outside the social, and so on.

We have mentioned the hippy and the technocrat and have seen how this false opposition can occur within a single family. Clouscard suggested differentiating the *standard of living* and the *lifestyle*. If, for example, the working-class lifestyle is directly tied to the standard of living, there exists little possibility for social mobility; for the bourgeoisie, on the other hand, multiple lifestyles can be promoted within a grandiose standard of living, which then leads to more confusion.

The bourgeoisie can be both, hippy and technocrat, ascetic and extravagant, right-wing and left-wing; it can embrace the "severe" father, De Gaulle, and the prodigal son, Cohn-Bendit.

Clouscard spoke also of "reciprocal engendering," or what might be called objective complicities. One of his most pertinent contributions was to have demonstrated the ideological matrix that generates those complicities, namely, neo-Kantianism: a term which takes on with Clouscard a more extensive meaning than that of the schools of Bade and of Marburg.

Indeed, we could say that it is the whole of bourgeois thinking that, in the best of cases, has stopped with Kant, with the *thing-in-itself*, with values, morality, and aesthetic; that which may be conceived of but not known; where the knowable field remains tied to the phenomenon, pertaining directly to the domain of the spirit and not of reason—of the so-called good engineer. For Clouscard, formalism sits on one side while empiricism sits on the other: Sartre's morality on one side and the implacability of structuralism on the other. In the text, *Critique of Libertarian Liberalism* (titled, in the past, *Rousseau or Sartre*), Clouscard argued against Sartre's unconditional freedom, stating that it was nothing else but the influence of structuralism within Marxism; whereas when Althusser spoke of "process without subject," according to Clouscard, history permitted the production of the subject (Cf. *Production of the Individual*). Clouscard's ambition consisted of a refusal of the Kantian dichotomy—*noumenon* and *phenomenon*—in order to propose a historical production of the transcendental subject, a historical production of human morality.

From the "District" to the New "Middle Classes"

To ratify tremendous political mutations, a *public* was required—namely, as Gramsci argued, a historical bloc made up, as in all times of reaction, by the alliance between the owning class and the so-called middle class. These middle strata would then be used to act as a buffer between those who hold capital and those who have nothing to lose but their chains.

The progressive liberalization of mores and customs facilitated a new market of desire of which the middle "class" became the first customers. Following this, market increases occurred to the benefit of the new emancipations promoted by the market itself.

Those middle strata, made up of generalized salaried workers, could no longer be defined by small-scale traditional ownership, or by simple ownership for that matter, but found themselves within a fully-fledged and well-established consumerist system where they existed as both market and advertisement. As such, it becomes more appropriate to speak of a *middle strata* than of a well-defined class in itself, primarily because those strata have the express function of *masking* the class struggle—the facing-off between worker and capitalist. The ideology of the middle strata is, frighteningly, the third way.

Clouscard described the complete mutation of the small, Poujadist,[1] petit bourgeois artisan into the generalized salaried worker, an agent of the non-productive economy and service industry. This, for Clouscard, represented a passage from local fascism (traditional extreme right) to *world fascism*; a fascism able, under the mask of social democracy, to starve people through the IMF, the World Bank, and to carry on racialized assaults on a global scale—as can be witnessed today with the processes of an on-going "re-colonization" of the world.

Prior to the emergence of monopolistic state capitalism, these middle strata remained *virtual*. That is, they remained subjected to matrix sectors of parliamentary and radical socialist management.

For Clouscard, the schoolteacher, the professor, and the attorney represented the three steps of the path from rural elite to urban culture. Secondary to the postwar transformation, these professions

---

1 **Editor's note:** Pierre Poujade (1920 - 2003) was a French politician after whom the 1950s Poujadist movement was named.

found some illusory autonomy. From being the agents of transmission, the clerk, the office employee, and the teacher had now become the prescribers and the decision makers. The middle strata had become homogenized.

The middle strata staunchly promote an extant and predetermined ideology. "Hollywood takes on the street," exclaimed Clouscard. This sentiment needs no further explaining. What needs explaining, however, is how this ideology spread—and to that end, one must appreciate the role of the district (*quartier*). Regarding the district, Clouscard addressed two different times and places that have affected French culture: namely surrealist *Montparnasse* and existentialist *Saint-Germain-des-pres*. The character of these districts emerged with the arrival of demographic surpluses, most notably marginalized children. They are characteristically and politically centrist (although believe themselves to be radical) in the sense that they not only refuse capitalism but socialism as well. Thus, they remain in between—able to reject the system yet unable to criticize it. Consequent to the district citizens' mundane lifestyles, they become part of an emergent mass culture, ultimately benefiting the existence of the new middle strata.

Clouscard's 1978 text, *The Frivolous and the Serious* articulated how the essentiality of the *dis-*

trict emerges from a culture of marginalized individuals of independent means able to establish selective and elitist scenes, cafes, salons, etc. while promoting its own type of coded, esoteric culture. As a result of its enculturation, this model comes ready-to-wear. The district becomes prescriptive of the model, the place of reference, which becomes prescriber of all and everything. "Place comes to be an image," Clouscard wrote, "a symbolic image, and model of the symbolic, normative model." The model spreads today as well through the internet. For instance, popular shows demonstrate to the countryside the how and why of libidinal, ludic, and marginal consumption, with their aesthetic emphases on beautiful district structures and nightlife.

1968 bore witness to the political utilization of this aestheticizing model. From Poujadist artisans to a great number of students, and from French citizens returning from Algeria to, namely, a whole demographic surplus, the system was only able to integrate within the new ideology the aesthetic of revolution, void of content. Petit-bourgeois masses and elites alike were synthesized, and "[u]nreal protest takes to the street." As Lucien Goldmann told Jacques Lacan, refuting the latter's structuralism to propose a synthesis with Marxism (that is, a genetic structuralism), "structures do not take to the streets." To this, Lacan had the easy answer that

May 68 proved, precisely, the exact opposite.

Without going all the way back to Hegel, one could observe in France the following evolution, from surrealism to existentialism, from the hippy movement to the "green" movement. Every time, French society attended a mass broadening of the evolutionary phenomenon in support of the *third way*. Unable to recognize their role in the process of production, these social types become terrified, not only of concrete political activity but also of progress and "technique." Whence the catastrophism, not stuck on specifics, from the club of Rome to today.

May 1968, Beginning of the *Reconquista*

These new social strata thought the party was only beginning, yet now, today, they exist in crisis. They believed that they had made the revolution their own—perhaps because they had achieved a small amount of social change; change that today's neo-puritanism, born from economic crisis, threatens to take away from them. A privilege had been mistaken for revolutionary emancipation.

This was May 1968—the July 14 of the new middle class. Even though there were clear social gains as workers were able to jump on the bandwagon, it is from this point that the "forty shameful years" of social regression began in France, all in the name of the "societal." The societal had imposed itself to hamper the social when it could have been its positive complement.

The decisive advances of the popular front, until the Grenelle accords, would become the object of an implacable *Reconquista* by capital and the socio-economic counter-revolution, within which, of course, the "left-wing" side of May 68 played a role as decisive as that of capital—as claimed by Daniel Cohn-Bendit, who stated that "Gaullo-communism [was] over," explicitly declaring himself a "liberal-libertarian," indirectly paying tribute to Clouscard who had, in fact, just coined the expression in 1972, in his text, *Neo-fascism and the Ideology of Desire*.

May 68, despite the significant social gains it allowed, must incite contemporary thinkers to make a critical appraisal *without* complacency. Indeed, it constituted a prophetic caesura between the decline of two great forces of *the resistance* and the return of Atlanticism, both right and left, from Mitterrand to Sarkozy.

Capitalism progressed with ever-greater energy to recoup the stuff left over from the Marshall Plan. Ever after, "[e]verything [was] allowed but nothing [was] possible." Emancipation could now be defined within an authorized and rigid frame of consumerism.

The crisis ratified the permissive model with the cultivation of yearning; making one miss it as though it was some lost paradise. Mundane consumption, libidinal, ludic, and marginal could then better approach the status of a founding mythology—a little like the famous, the rock stars, who could ultimately do no better than dying in order to be worshiped by their fans. This phenomenon first created the need, then it organized the lack.

In the meantime, capitalism, destroyed the material supports of the French republican spirit, and "[brought] the civil war amongst the poor"— namely the confrontation born from the overcrowding of working-class districts, between the sub-proletariat and the proletariat, between the French immigrant workers and foreign immigrant workers, between the unemployed and the worker. Everything operated to conceal popular culture, to prevent the reconstitution of the popular front. This was a time of incommunicability, the absence of all mediations, a time of vengeful frustrations, of those wishing for their slice of the cake.

Everything was set up for the rise of a new fascism.

Popular Resistance

Some may share such observations of overall general alienation and, at this point, stop their reflection, in some complacent despair; but Clouscard never fell into this fatalism. He could be registered in the lineage of the great thinkers of determinism, from Spinoza to Marx, and even Freud in some ways—determinist and non-mechanistic—for they never denied human freedom, yet they defined it, however, as with Spinoza, as the "intellection of necessity," and speak, along with Marx, of "trend determinism." Moral freedom, a freedom which is not given, but a lengthy conquest, must, in the end, break down social determinisms. Accordingly, Clouscard had proposed, far from the Sartrean moral duty of existence, a concrete morality of engagement.

Clouscard did not forget that the fundamental contradiction of capitalist society was, before all else, a contradiction between capital and labor—namely that it was a given, entailed by capitalist modes of production, that it would always pertain to it. Hence, Clouscard's loyalty to the side of the workers, and his support of the Communist Party, which represented the party of the collectivity—of the class opposed to capital. This positionality clearly distinguished Clouscard from the great thinkers of his time; those who were often seduced by extreme leftism (and we have clarified the mundane prestige obtained from such position). Clouscard's contradistinction from these thinkers explains, in part, the relative silence of the intelligentsia regarding his work, with the remarkable exception of Henry Lefebvre who saw in Clouscard an interlocutor of choice.

Clouscard's work did have an echo in milieus close to the Communist Party, bringing the benefit of getting the decisive support of *Editions Sociales*, the publishing house of the Party. It was clear that at the time that Clouscard thought he could play a key role in the elaboration of a efficient response 1) to thwart the strategy of neocapitalism, that is to say, of libertarian social democracy, and 2) to analyze the new condition of the working world to be re-conquered. Clouscard's work introduced a form of applied Marxism, rigorous and complex, as it refused the dogmatism fed by imageries and identitarianism while giving up Marxisms mired in over-quantification and opportunism. The debate typical of Clouscard's time over the acceptance or rejection of the "dictatorship of the proletariat," had led to the specular intensification of both tendencies, when it could have allowed for a concrete analysis of the concrete situation of the world of labor.

Some have reproached the Communist Party for its failure to address the question of the middle classes. This was the observation formulated by Party's historian, Roger Martelli, close to the current of "re-foundation." In my opinion, the question was poorly put. There is always the necessity to create class alliances, and middle classes are essential in that they can go one way or the other. But this does not mean they are the only ones voting, or that they alone must be courted, seduced into the strategy of libertarian liberalism, which, it can be said, always ends up with a divorce of the middle classes from the laboring class.

Without pretending to anticipate the decisions of an imagined headquarters neglecting to teach lessons to their comrades, we must, on the contrary, become aware of the organizing role of the *whole world of labor* and thereby propose concrete conditions for a path towards socialism.

The foundering of world communism, which was not, in fact, implicated in the historical collapse of the French Communist Party—given that it started doing so decades prior, and that, in comparison, other communist parties around the world and in Europe have fared much better—has been used as alibi in order not to address the actual causes of the decline of the Party that has contributed to the postwar construction of this country, particularly since the Popular Front. If the Communist Party was, for Gramsci, the "modern prince," like between Machiavelli and Laurent the Magnificent, there was, between Clouscard and the Communist Party, a missed rendezvous. Only the future will be able to tell whether such an historical mistake will be mended or not.

Whatever it may be, Michel Clouscard did bear witness of a kind of popular resistance to the totalitarian dictatorship of the new market. Clouscard provided, theoretically, the equivalent of what Pasolini did for poetic verse. In the end, a great popular laughter must overcome the mockery that is the libertarian liberal society. As Hegel demonstrated, the *people* must climb on stage.

We find with Clouscard an intervention shaped like a sociology—or, rather, a kind of novella without characters, or a novella with ideal-types but without intrigue. Clouscard wrote the story of the disappearance of fiction. In that way, he avoided the neo-scientism of those social sciences so consecrated in the 60s, with the triumphal technocracy, and after the issue of the Algerian war. The fiction novel in which "the Marquise went out at 5 o'clock" is no longer true for the descriptive novel; it must remain anecdotal.

In Clouscard's work, we find Marx—but we also find Moliere and Balzac. France is the great nation of literature, or, to be more precise, the place where literature fulfills its theoretical and political potentials, and it is certainly not happenstance that modern Marxism was assembled in France.

Clouscard is more novelist than sociologist. This is because, as a Marxist, he refused the scientific assumptions that had presided over the birth of sociology. Let us remember that Marx despised August Comte but loved Balzac, a fact that the representatives of "socialist realism" would do well to remember.

Clouscard was not only interested in ideology but also in its anthropological buttresses (even though he remained quite aware that politics and psyche were not in an immediate relationship of expression, and that numerous mediations, in fact, intervened). It is because Clouscard was a good philosopher that he became a novelist—perhaps in order to shape a type of anthropological *path* (here, Hegel would have said a "phenomenology of mind") for the categories of mind and sensibility.

Being, knowledge, and the subject itself are attributes of history, of the general process of production. It is on this precise point that one might be inclined to speak, with Clouscard, of a Hegelian radicalization of Marxism.

Anxious to offer efficient modeling, Clouscard did not hesitate to show, for instance, that if there were not thirty-six modes of productions, then there were not, either, thirty-six forms of psyche.

Clouscard articulated four fundamental modes: the Middle Ages mythical, the sentimental romanticism of the bourgeoisie, the libido of psychoanalysis, and the sexuality of libertarian liberalism. It is the praxis that begets the psyche, exclaimed Clouscard, contrary to what psychoanalysis would tell us; that is, a psychoanalysis that believed in "natural" drives. Clouscard's ultimate point was that there was no desire that existed before the relationships of production; that production produced desire.

Clouscard was, above all, a theorist of *psyche*—psyche as an *instance* born from praxis. The latter set up all the mediations necessary for the emergence of psyche—or its repression. Because of Clouscard, we are free to exit the scholastic opposition between materialism and idealism, an opposition which never got beyond the point of view of a vulgar materialism already denounced by Marx.

There is a necessity, if we are to be true to a veritable critique of political economy, to reconstitute an aesthetics, an ethics, and all the categories of the psyche. Tying praxis and psyche, Clouscard ended up suggesting a transitory morality, founded on production—an ethics immanent in the mode of production. The only "viable" political morality, for Clouscard, must be articulated around these notions. It could not proceed from dogmatism or from some abstract imperative; it must be bound to production. In other words, "[y]ou will not consume more than you produce." Michel Clouscard found the meaning of civic engagement anchored in a concrete universality—of a Marxism incarnated into the republican reality of France.

www.ingramcontent.com/pod-product-compliance
Lightning Source LLC
Chambersburg PA
CBHW030459010526
44118CB00011B/1020